LEON KIRCHNER

PIANO SONATA NO. 2

*The first performance of PIANO SONATA No. 2
was given by Russell Sherman on 2 November 2003
at the Isabella Stewart Gardner Museum,
Boston, Massachusetts.*

*A recording by Jeremy Denk
is available on Albany Records: Troy 906*

duration ca. 14 minutes

AMP 8202
First Printing: October 2013

ISBN 978-1-4234-0782-9

Associated Music Publishers, Inc.

DISTRIBUTED BY
HAL•LEONARD®
CORPORATION
7777 W. BLUEMOUND RD. P.O. BOX 13819 MILWAUKEE, WI 53213

for Ralph Berkowitz

PIANO SONATA No. 2

Leon Kirchner

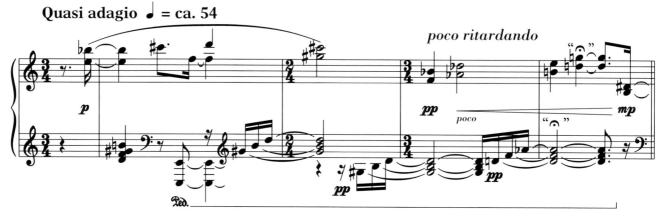

Steady, un poco meno mosso
♪ = 160

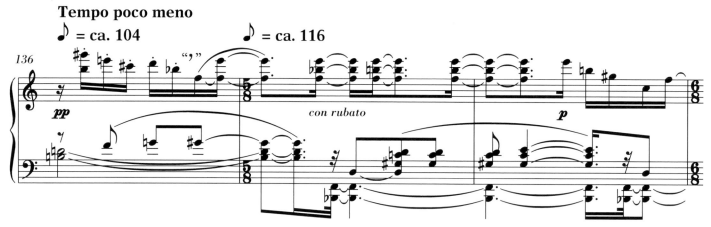

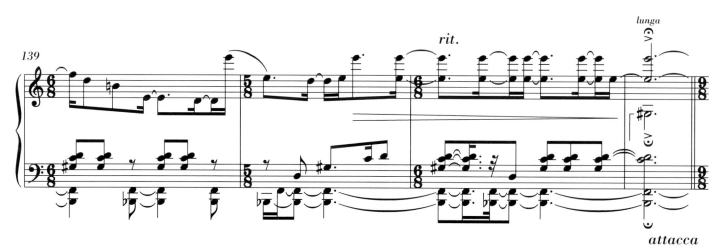

attacca

With great flexibility ♩ = 48+

Quasi cadenza

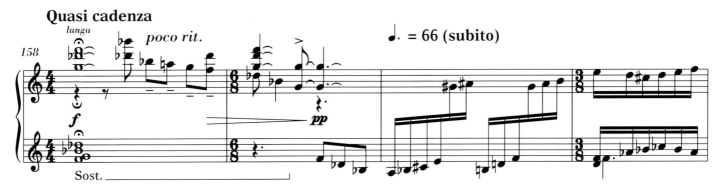

Subito meno mosso

al tempo ♪ = 160

Slower tempo subito
♪ = 92

riten.

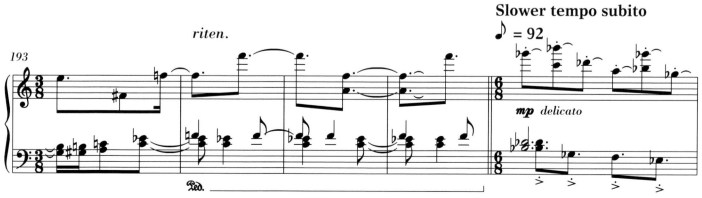

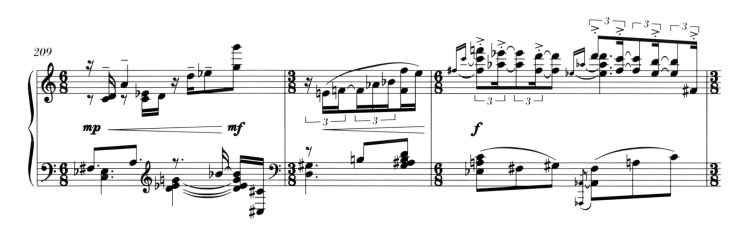

20

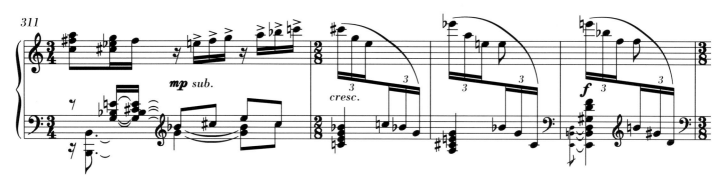

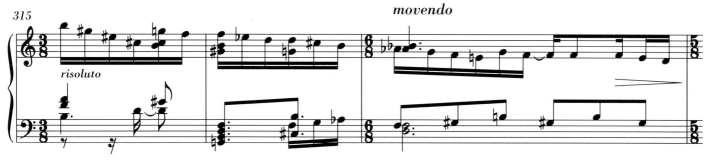

Più mosso ♩ = 92,

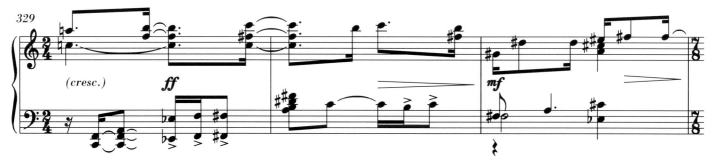

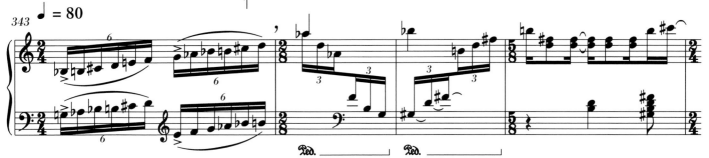

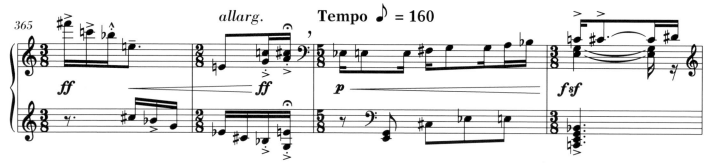

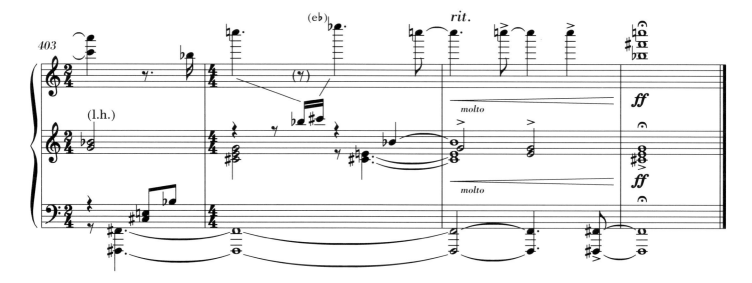